369 0299973

THE SYSTEMS THINKING TOOLKIT

KT-444-949

MONKLANDS HOSPITAL
LIBRARY
MONKSCOURT AVENUE
AIRDRIE ML60JS
L C1236712005

Other books in this series:

*For a complete list of Management Books 2000 titles
visit our web-site on http://www.mb2000.com*

THE SYSTEMS THINKING TOOLKIT

Stuart Emmett

2000

BARCODE NO: 36902 99973
CLASS NO: W26.5 EMM.
PRICE: 6.99
DATE: 23|12|14.

*This book is dedicated to my family – to my wife, the lovely Christine,
to our two cute children, Jill and James, and James's wife, Mairead
(also cute), and to our totally gorgeous three granddaughters, twins
Megan and Molly and their younger sister, Niamh.*

MONKLANDS HOSPITAL
LIBRARY
MONKSCOURT AVENUE
AIRDRIE ML60JS
01236712005

Copyright © Stuart Emmett 2008, 2010

All rights reserved. No part of this publication may be reproduced, stored in a
retrieval system, or transmitted in any form or by any means, electronic,
mechanical, photocopying, recording, or otherwise without the prior permission of
the publishers.

First published in 2008 by Management Books 2000 Ltd

This new edition published in 2010 by Management Books 2000 Ltd
Forge House, Limes Road
Kemble, Cirencester
Gloucestershire, GL7 6AD, UK
Tel: 0044 (0) 1285 771441
Fax: 0044 (0) 1285 771055
Email: info@mb2000.com
Web: www.mb2000.com

This book is sold subject to the condition that it shall not, by way of trade or
otherwise, be lent, resold, hired out, or otherwise circulated without the publisher's
prior consent in any form of binding or cover other than that in which it is published
and without a similar condition including this condition being imposed upon the
subsequent purchaser.

British Library Cataloguing in Publication Data is available

ISBN 9781852526610

AUTHOR'S NOTE

In writing this book, I have made best-efforts endeavours not to include anything that, if used, would be injurious or cause financial loss to the user. The user is, however, strongly recommended, before applying or using any of the contents, to check and verify their own company policy/requirements. No liability will be accepted for the use of any of the contents.

It can also happen in a lifetime of learning and meeting people, that the original source of an idea or information has been forgotten. If I have actually omitted in this book to give anyone credit they are due, I do apologise and hope they will make contact so I can correct the omission in future editions.

CONTENTS

INTRODUCTION

Welcome to this new series of business toolkits designed to improve personal and work performance.

A recent report entitled "The Missing Millions – how companies mismanage their most valuable resource" (source: www.Proudfootconsulting.com) stated that "Poor management in the UK is directly responsible for 60 lost working days per employee per year. And a further 25 days lost annually can also be indirectly attributed to management failing."

That is a total of 85 wasted days per employee every year due to poor and failing management. This is around 30% of a normal working year of 240 available days!

According to the report, the main contributing factors were as follows:

- Insufficient planning and control
- Inadequate supervision
- Poor morale
- Inappropriate people development
- IT related problems

- Ineffective communication

This series of concise guides will provide practical advice in each of these key management areas, to enable managers to get the most out of their teams, and make sure that they stay ahead of the game.

The simple truth is that in order to avoid the incredible 85 wasted days per employee per year referred to above, things must be done better *by management*.

Problems with management will almost always turn out to be people problems. Improving performance is therefore essentially about improving individual and team performance so that, in turn, the organisation's performance is improved.

This will require that, for example, the following are considered:

- Developing a strong strategic vision that is underpinned with learning
- Motivating and developing and releasing the potential of people, as individuals and in teams
- Communicating to people what is expected, what they are rewarded for, how they should deliver results and what results the organisation is looking for.

The earlier mentioned Proudfoot research highlighted several areas that managers can work on to improve performance. These are shown again below with a link to the appropriate Toolkit:

- Insufficient planning and control – dealt with in this Systems Thinking Toolkit
- Inadequate supervision – see the Team Management Toolkit
- Poor morale – see the Motivation Toolkit
- Inappropriate people development – see the Developing People Toolkit
- IT related problems – dealt with in this Systems Thinking Toolkit
- Ineffective communication – see the Communication Toolkit

It should be appreciated that many of these aspects do inter-relate, and that a single quick fix in one area may not always work very well. The Systems Thinking Toolkit does examine more fully all of the interconnected links of inputs, processes and outputs to be considered when improving performance. Also, the Learning Toolkit is paramount, as improvements can only be made after making changes and change, in turn, is directly associated to new learning.

As we have seen, many of the Proudfoot research aspects are directly people-related. In addition to the specific toolkits mentioned above, the Human Resources Toolkit provides a complete framework for effective human resources management.

Finally, as we all know, no business can survive without customers, and the essential skills of customer service are absolutely vital to the retention and growth of the customer base. The Customer Service Toolkit provides quick and easy advice which will produce startling returns.

PART 1
UNDERSTANDING
PERFORMANCE

1

WHAT IS PERFORMANCE?

This series of Toolkits is all about improving performance – but what *is* Performance? Let's start with a diagram that illustrates the general business process:

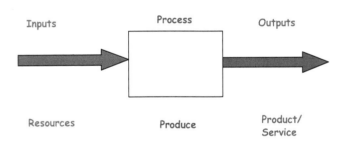

Inputs	Process	Outputs
Resources	Produce	Product/ Service

The performance of the product or service output is determined by the process that produced it. In turn, the process will depend upon the input of resources, such as the usage of money, time, equipments, materials, methods of working and the people (as individuals, groups and teams).

So we need to have inputs of resources into a process, before we can have a performance output.

The input of resources, the process production, and the output of products or services are all connected and interlinked. They constitute a process which may be defined as a sequence of dependent events, involving time, which has a valued result for the eventual end user.

As all of these aspects are related, it follows that we cannot improve performance without considering the process and methods used, and the resources utilised in the process.

2

PERFORMANCE MEASUREMENT

The output or the performance can be measured, by looking at what we expected against what we obtained, and the input or the utilisation of resources can be measured, by seeing what was used against what available.

The complete method of calculating these measurements can be seen in the following diagram:

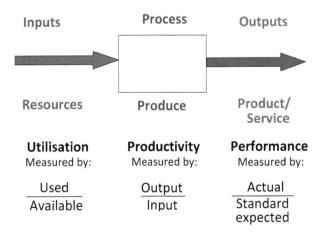

Inputs	Process	Outputs
Resources	Produce	Product/ Service
Utilisation Measured by:	**Productivity** Measured by:	**Performance** Measured by:
$\dfrac{\text{Used}}{\text{Available}}$	$\dfrac{\text{Output}}{\text{Input}}$	$\dfrac{\text{Actual}}{\text{Standard}}$ expected

3

PERFORMANCE IMPROVEMENT

If the output, or the performance, does not match the standard expected, then we can generate feedback to change the process or the inputs, so that we can then get the exact output wanted.

The following diagram illustrates these feedback loops

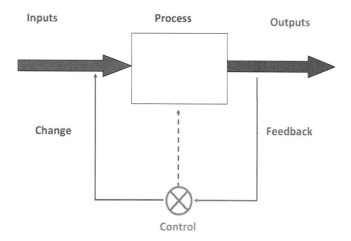

Inputs and processes can be changed by responses to feedback loops; these are at the heart of how we can improve any performance. They are also, as we will see soon, fundamental to systems thinking.

4

MANAGE ON THE LEFT SIDE

As has been seen, inputs-process-outputs are all connected. An important point with performance measurement is that the measurement is always going to be after the product and service has been delivered and completed; the vast majority of performance measurement will always be time-lagged.

For example, management accounts compare what we expected or budgeted for, against what has been actually spent. Although the budgets themselves may be prepared before the expenditure, the accounts which measure actual performance will inevitably be prepared *after* the expenditure has already been incurred.

Effective performance management means recognising *in advance* just what are the key inputs that affect the process and the outputs. Then, later, we can measure how we have best utilised the inputs for a given output. If we do this correctly, this will automatically mean that there are no performance output surprises.   As performance will always be directed towards customers, (internal or external), then it is critically important that we get the performance output to customers right. (Customer Service is more fully explored in the Customer Service Toolkit).

Meanwhile, if the output is not one that is required, then the process will need examining. Maybe we are doing things wrong; maybe there is a better way. Maybe we have to change the process, and also the inputs; we may have to change the whole system. This is real proactive performance management and we can do this by what I call "managing on the left side".

This managing on the left side is not only simple conceptually, but is also simple in practice. It seems to be plain common sense, but then, as has been said, it may be sense, but it is not very common. Unfortunately, the relationship and the connection between the inputs and the output are often just not seen by managers.

For example, many organisations and managers wait for the delayed output performance measures before they will change anything; this is a classic example of reactive management. This is also not helped by the common use of what are known as "key performance indicators" (KPIs) that will only ever tell us what we have done, after we actually have done it.

5

PROACTIVE PERFORMANCE

Just as important as KPIs are what are known as KUIs (key utilisation indicators). As we have seen, a key measure of proper process management is the measurement of utilisation. Utilisation can be assessed at an early stage, and, in turn, it is the utilisation which works through to affect the performance. KUI's will therefore tell us, diagnostically, why something will not perform. A very simple operational example will highlight the use of KPI's and KUI's:

Example

A warehouse despatch department has two fork trucks and two drivers per shift who load pallets onto road vehicles.

The KPI on number of pallets delivered/loaded from a warehouse was measured as follows:

<u>No. of pallets actually loaded per shift</u>
No. of pallets expected to be loaded per shift

On one work shift this worked out at 15,000/30,000 pallets, giving 50% performance of pallets loaded per shift.

This KPI is affected by many things – for example, the process used for despatch, the use and availability of vehicles to load to, and the information, labour and equipment etc.

The KUI for the utilisation of fork lift truck equipment was measured as follows:

<u>Fork truck hours used per shift</u>
Fork truck hours available per shift

On this particular work shift this worked out at 10/20 hours, giving 50% utilisation of fork lift truck hours per shift

The KUI for labour utilisation (drivers of fork lift trucks) was measured as follows:

<u>At work</u>
Expected at work

On this work shift, this KUI worked out at 1 / 2 giving a 50% absenteeism measure.

Comments:

This shows how KUIs can explain the KPI.

In this very simple operational example, we hope a manager overseeing this activity would have known at the start of the shift, that one person was absent and would then have arranged for a replacement. Hopefully, they would not have waited for the KPI at the end of the shift to reveal the low performance.

This simple example illustrates the critical message that inputs relate to outputs and by managing the inputs, we get an early warning of performance problems and therefore can manage pro-actively. We do not need to wait for the performance measurement to tell us something needs changing.

This need for proactive rather than reactive management has also been noted by Nick Read, CEO of Vodaphone UK, who says that "what most managers are doing is not leading but managing retrospectively what has already happened in the business" (Sunday Times, 1 April 2007).

Read continues with the following comment of how time is managed by leaders and managers:

Agenda	% Time spent	% Time spent

	should be	usually is
People, (staff, workers)	40%	20%
Customers	40%	20%
Results	20%	60%

The link between inputs and outputs is also a classic example of causal thinking. Potentially there can be multiple causes and this, as will see, is an important aspect of systems thinking.

6

PERFORMANCE AND PROCESSES

We have earlier defined a process as "a sequence of dependant events, involving time, which has a valued result for the eventual end user".

Processes are, so often, selected portions of larger streams of activities that are:

- transformational (they convert inputs to outputs)

  and/or:

- transactional (they exchange outputs for new inputs, thus giving feedback into the process)

This is especially important when considering improvements and whether to change the process and/or change the inputs.

The other important aspect, when considering performance improvements to any process, is to understand the three key features of processes; dependencies, variabilities and interfaces. It is usually these key features that will actually determine how well or not the process performs.

Looking at each of these in turn we can see the following characteristics:

Dependencies

- Receive inputs and changes them to outputs
- Are those sequential and related "knock on effects"
- What happens "here" causes events "there" – for example, consumer demand triggers many varied supply chain networks
- "A" may need to be finished before "B" can start
- Any process is only as efficient as its most inefficient part –for example, "a chain is as strong as its weakest link"
- The most important factor to manage is therefore the most limiting one

Variabilities

- Variability is when the "fixed, known and expected" can become "variable, unknown and unexpected" – for example, expected demand changes to be random demand

- They can causes changes from a state of "certainty" to a state of "uncertainty"
- Each part with variability can causes knock-on effects, with sometimes catastrophic results
- Statistical measures, (e.g. normal distribution curve), can often be used to measure the variabilities of technical systems
- However, people's hopes and aspirations are also a variable – and are often the most important one (see The Motivation Toolkit on how to improve motivation)

Interfaces

- Are the potential friction points between processes
- Are often ignored, as our minds concentrate on "the box" and only on what happens in the box
- How we make connections at the interfaces is therefore often ignored
- However, real dependencies also exist at the interface – not the least of which are people relationships and how the people involved connect cognitively

What happens often, however, is that we fail to fully appreciate all of the input/process/output connections with their dependencies, variabilities and interfaces.

To use the jargon, we can then sub-optimise. This is where we only look at one part of the whole, and this is usually the part making the most noise. This maybe correct, but so often it is not. When it is not and we change something, (in reality it is then the wrong thing), we then make the problem noise louder. This may also give a catastrophic outcome.

7

SYSTEMS THINKING

Enter therefore systems thinking, a brave approach to ensure that we look at "wholes" or take the holistic approach. Systems thinking has had a relatively recent history, with the following important milestones:

- Pre 1900s: Feedback control in engineering (the above input/output diagram is an example) – this introduced the feedback principle
- 1950s: Operational research – this started to use computing power to undertake "what if" analysis from varying the connections
- 1960s: Systems dynamics – Forrester and MIT were the main movers here and the book "Limits to Growth" is a classic that shows the complexity of inputs and variables on outputs
- 1970s: Soft systems – Checkland and the Open University developed the thinking into Human Activity systems

- 1990s: Learning organisations – Senge and his classic book "The Fifth Dimension" introduced the systems connections into organisations and the need for a learning organisation that continually reinvents itself

8

SYSTEMS, PROCESSES AND STRUCTURES

Processes do things in conjunction with **structures**; these are the fixed settings that include things like rules and procedures, organisational charts and formal culture. Structures have a powerful influence on how people behave and how things work in organisations. The interaction of structure with processes becomes interesting:

Structures are mainly	Processes are mainly
Stable and fixed settings	Transient and variable interactions
Supporting and containing; yet can also, constrain and limit	Building up and making; yet can also, break down/fragment and be defensive

Viewed as being independent, certain and self sufficient	Involving dependencies, variabilities and interfaces
Bringers of stability and certainty	Forcing change to accommodate the dependencies and variabilities

It is the working together of structure and process that creates a system, as shown by the following diagram:

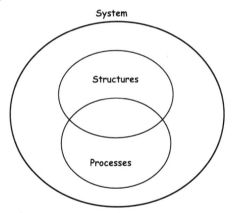

The interplay between structure and processes is critical to performance; and when making improvements, it is ultimately the behaviour of the overall system that we will have to improve. If processes and structures are both changed, then the behaviour will inevitably change.

PART 2
WHAT IS A SYSTEM?

9

DEFINITION

Some definitions of a system follow:

"A system is a group of interacting, interrelated and interdependent parts that form a complex and unified organised whole that does something. The behaviour of the system changes if any of the parts leave the system. It is the interaction of the parts, not the actions taken separately, that is essential. "

"A system is a dynamic and complex whole that has information flowing between its interacting parts and its environment. Whilst the system may seek equilibrium, it can exhibit oscillation, chaos or exponential growth/decay"

We live in a complex world. We are part of this world, and, paradoxically, the world in turn is part of us. Systems thinking reflects this paradox as the parts and the whole are entirely interdependent: the parts are in the whole, and the whole is in the parts.

A system has **a purpose,** and for optimum performance all elements or parts must be present and must be arranged in a specific way. This arranged way will change when we require a different performance.

Additionally, systems will **change in response to feedback**. Systems generally will attempt to maintain stability and control the system performance by making adjustments based on feedback (e.g. the kettle thermostat, or a hot body temperature that creates sweat).

A system is therefore an entity that maintains its existence and functions through the **interaction of its parts**. The behaviour of a system depends on how the parts are related, rather than just on the parts themselves; it is therefore about thinking in "wholes" and not just with the "parts."

Because systems are about **connections between wholes**, analysing or writing about them has some special difficulties. We do need to break things into parts to explain them, but in so doing, we must be careful not to lose sight of the whole.

We also have systems that are part of larger sub-systems and are composed of smaller systems; the more complex the system, then the more difficulties are found due to variability, dependency and the interfaces. Systems are often complex in the detail and in the dynamics.

To explain the workings of complex systems it is helpful to consider different types of system in terms of binary "Extremes" and "Ideal-Typical" views ("hard" and "soft", "formal" and "informal", and so on). These present polarised black-and-white views; the reality and the practice in organisations will generally be found in the "grey" area between the black-and-white extremes.

10

HARD AND SOFT SYSTEMS

We can identify two basic and general types of systems, hard and soft.

Hard systems are:

- Technical and engineered systems
- Generally predictable
- Quantifiable, tangible and objective (like money and products)

Soft systems are mainly what this Toolkit is concerned with and are:

- Organisation and human activity systems
- Complex and uncertain as they deal with behaviour, emotions, feelings, values, attitudes, politics, cultures
- Qualitative, intangible and subjective

To examine the hard and soft aspects further, I would commend to you the approach of Jack Welch, former chairman of GE USA, who viewed organisational systems in terms of "small within big." (Source: Welch's autobiography, "Jack: straight from the gut"). Jack Welch has had a powerful leadership voice in the last two decades and his views are important and influential.

"Small within big" is how I, personally, have always preferred to work, where there is a small number of people who need to be closely led and managed, but with the support from the wider and larger organisation on things like finance, research etc.

Welch describes the small and the big in an organisation as follows:

"Big" represents the hard values at the centre with

- technical support
- financial support
- managerial support

This is what Welch sees as the central and common culture.

"Small" represents the soft values at the sharp end:

- Reality – working with the way it is and not the way we wished it was
- Quality – each person is proud of what they do
- People – creating an atmosphere where people dare to try new things

This is seen as the freedom and flexible culture.

I do like these hard and soft comparisons, and to my mind it is irrefutable that the soft values are the ones that really count. It is the soft values that make the difference to organisations as they work directly on, and into, the people. And it is always people who do make the difference.

It is the soft values that "bring it home" at the front end, where it matters.

However, in spite of the use of the word "soft", this soft stuff is actually *hard* to do.

Why is the soft stuff hard? Well, it's because management is not at all only about hard scientific approaches but is, according to none other than Sir John Harvey-Jones, more about being an art:

> "In my view, management is not so much a science, as an art. It is an art because management consists of enlisting the freely given support of disparate groups of people at different times to achieve, by their own free will, an agreed common purpose."
>
> Sir John Harvey-Jones

Sound words of wisdom indeed.

In the context of this hard/soft divide, I am also very aware of some current and popular financially-driven management beliefs such as:

> *"The only thing that counts is the financial bottom line"*

> *"Achieving the financial targets are all that matters."*

For too many leaders and managers, these are the ultimate truths in their organisations, and "the financials" are pursued relentlessly and without compromise.

The simple truth however, is that it is the "soft" people who will make any of the "hard" financial differences. So, by ensuring the effective use of people as the main inputs and drivers in an organisation, then the hard financial outputs must follow.

11

DANGERS OF USING ONLY HARD VALUES

"Hard" values measurement, alone, is dangerous. It will be found that this often gives totally inappropriate standards for an organisation's total performance which will inevitably bring failure in the medium to longer term, as the soft values are being subordinated and ignored; yet it is actually these soft values that will drive the organisation to meet its hard values.

We do need both soft and hard values.

I fear, for example, that most of the target-setting in Government bureaucracies and in the UK National Health Service uses totally inappropriate standards of performance based only on hard values. Control and regulation seems to have taken over by using only some of the standards that are available. The other standards are ignored.

When "hard value" standards alone are focused

on some of the parts in a holistic integrated system, then "there will be trouble ahead".

When focusing on parts only, the whole is not considered and in looking only at the parts, then the purpose and meaning for the whole is lost. Simple really, but not at all well understood. In trying to control only the output actions from what I call the human *doing* (see page 65), we may now find that we have lost the essential human *being*.

> "The whole concept of management in Britain has been debased by being seen as synonymous with control and regulation."
>
> Sir John Harvey-Jones

Control is only one aspect of management, concerned with planning, organising, coordination and control of processes and individuals. When hard values and systems controls are the primary (or exclusive) methods being used to run an organisation, the achievement of the corresponding key performance indicators becomes all that matters.

Then ultimately, the people in the organisation will only do what is required to be done – i.e. whatever is directed by the control measurement. Most people will only do what they are going to be measured on, as doing this determines their "carrot or stick" work performance rewards. (To examine rewards and motivation more fully, please see The Motivation Toolkit).

Therefore, if an organisation is measuring the wrong things, the work will be wrong. The people will eventually suffer as they will not be doing the right things and this, in turn, can lead to extra cost and eventual failure. When this is "discovered" later – and it will be later, as the performance measures being used are reactive ones – then the fault, with attendant blame, will be attributed to the people working within the organisations.

If, as a result of this inappropriate measurement policy, some sub-optimal changes have been made to meet the measurement target, it may now be some years later before the system is seen to not work. Now, whilst it will be still be considered the fault of the people, it will also be recognised as a fault of the system.

Time meanwhile has passed, and those who originated the use of hard measurements only will not realise, or at worse will choose to forget, that they were cause of the problem in the first place.

For those who may find that this critique on using only hard drivers and measurements clashes with their management training and experiences, then there is a real learning lesson here – simply, that all leaders and managers need to ensure that the entire organisation is actively promoting, above everything else, the soft values and the soft skills in the art of management.

And for those who still need convincing, four quotes follow from Peter Drucker:

"Organisations do not exist for their own sake. The organisations goal is a specific contribution to individual and society. The test of its performance lies outside of itself."

"The task of management is to make people capable of joint performance, to make their strengths effective and their weaknesses irrelevant."

"The business enterprise is a system of the highest order; a system whose parts are human beings contributing voluntarily of their knowledge, skill and dedication to a joint venture."

"To manage a business is to balance a variety of needs and goals. To emphasise only profit, misdirects managers to the point where they may endanger the survival of the business."

Source: Peter Drucker

We must ensure that the right choices are made about the relative importance of hard and soft values in the structures and processes of an organisation. As noted earlier in Part 1, if processes and structures are changed, the behaviour will inevitably change. It is therefore totally appropriate that the organisational culture or "the way we do things around here" is consciously considered.

The culture will therefore need careful planning/design, organising/implementing and controlling/monitoring, so that all of the principles we have discussed so far are effectively delivered.

Getting this company culture "right" is considered next.

PART 3
ORGANISATIONAL CULTURE

People working for specific companies find that they have their own way of doing things. For example, people who leave one company to join another company to do a similar job must soon appreciate the urgent and early need to fit into their new company – whilst they will be technically competent, they will also now need to be, culturally competent.

A company has its own culture, which we can define as "the way we do things around here".

12

BLAME CULTURE

The following quote from Peter Drucker indicates what he sees as one unfortunate aspect of culture:

> "Insecurity – not economic but psychological insecurity - permeates the entire industrial situation. It creates fear; and since it is fear of the unknown and the unpredictable, it leads to a search for scapegoats and culprits".
>
> Peter Drucker

Here the inherently created fear would create a blame culture. If there is a blame culture – and there are many – then the changing of a company culture will need to pass through the following "ideal-typical" stages:

Aspect	"Stormy/Blame" Culture	"Steady/Sane" Culture	"Sunny/Gain" Culture
Goals	Announced	Communicated	Agreed
Information	Status symbol and power based	Traded	Abundant
Motivation	Manipulative	Focused on staff needs	A clear goal and expected
Decisions	From above	Partly delegated	Staff make most
Mistakes	Are only made by staff	Responsibility is taken	Are allowed as learning lessons
Conflicts	Are unwelcome and "put down"	Are mastered	Are a source of new innovation
Control	From above	Partly delegated	Fully delegated
Management Style	Authoritarian/ aggressive	Cooperative	Participative/ Assertive
Authority	Requires obedience	Requires cooperation	Requires collaboration
Manager is	Absolute ruler. Feels superior	Problem-solver and decision-maker	Change strategist. Self-confident

Culture will be shown formally and informally, as the culture of an organisation provides the central atmosphere which the people operate in. Some aspects will be formal and overt; some will be more informal and possibility more covert.

13

FORMAL AND INFORMAL CULTURES

Formal Culture

Company culture can be shown by the published vision, mission and goals, and in the rules, norms and procedures of a company – such formal statements providing a hard, factual and objective view of an organisation's culture.

In fact, the formal structure of a company culture may be seen in all public statements made by the company. Public statements may be said to give an *overt* demonstration of the company culture – for example,

1) Vision, Mission and Goals/Objectives statements, where we find that:

- The vision incorporates those timeless values and beliefs that are intended to move an organisation to its required future. They are an image of what it is trying to do; they represent the future required reality. They should come from the inside of people, but when they do not, the vision statement will be superficial and mere hollow statements of hopes and desires.

- The mission incorporates the purpose, policies, and power structures to achieve the task.
- The goals are the strategic, tactical and operational objectives, right down to people's individual roles and responsibilities.

The above statements should be used to lead and manage the efficient running on the company; they will give the overall direction, guidance and "checkpoints". They should therefore not be lofty inspiring statements of vague intent, but must be practically expressed and lived out. When used this way, they must also become internalised by the people in the organisation.

2) Rules and procedures statements

Rules are very structural as they represent pre-set standards of conduct and show the way people should behave by clarifying what is expected of them. Procedures, in turn, are written to help people keep to the rules and to establish the methods to be used. Procedures maintain and apply the rules or standards, so that they give, and show, a fair and consistent approach. They will also, providing they are so written, bring clarity. Rules and procedures are therefore structurally built into organisations.

Of course, just publishing formal statements carries no guarantees whatsoever that the statements will determine or influence the way that things are actually done. Indeed, when introducing a new mission or vision statement, it seems there is often a corporate arrogance. Introductions and launches are here accompanied with much pomp and PR of a one-sided view, which has often made no effective attempt to get any "buy-in" from the people in the organisation.

Informal Culture

Culture is also often covert and informal, with values and beliefs that can remain undefined. This is the more subjective aspect of culture. For example, contrast the difference between a charity and a private sector organisation, between an army platoon and a football team, between the civil service and a retailer, between the Royal Mail and DHL.

As well as things like clothing styles, office styles and the types of buildings, differences will also be found in the human "software" represented by the attitudes, values, and beliefs that operate behind the scenes and below the visible surface.

Informal culture is similar to the body language in face-to-face communication; we can be subjectively and unconsciously influenced by it. Leaders and managers will ignore the informal culture at their peril. It is often not the published statements that provide an organisation's direction; it can be that the informal cultures that are actually in the driving seat.

14

TOTAL CULTURE

In all forms of management there are, as earlier discussed at length, the hard, objective and clearly defined ways of managing, and also those more subjective beliefs, values and soft skills.

An overall and complete view of culture needs to embody the hard and soft aspects into all of the following:

1) Purpose:

- What are the objectives, procedures and rules?
- What are the supporting structures?
- What are the supporting processes?

These explain the "why?" and the "what do we do and how?" of the organisation.

2) Power:

- Who has access to which resources?
- Where is the central and the decentralised authority?

This is the "where and when?" of decision making in the organisation.

3) People:

- What is the degree of support and trust?
- What is valued?
- What are the associated reward structures?

This is the "with who?" and the "how?" of the organisation.

It maybe that **Purpose** and **Power** are easier to change than the **People** beliefs, attitudes and behaviour of the individuals of the company culture. Whilst all of these three parts are interwoven, it is however only these soft "people" aspects which will really make the difference and ultimately represent the main differentiator between organisations.

As we have already noted, the simple truth is that it is the "soft" people who will make the "hard" financial differences. In cultural terms "soft" and "hard" systems translate to "friendly" and "unfriendly" cultures, as illustrated in the table below. You can assess the friendliness or unfriendliness of an organisation by observing and talking to the people in the company, to get an indication of just how the people aspects are actually working.

Friendly ☺	Unfriendly ☹
People take the initiative	People feel boxed in
Teamwork flourishes	Friction and a lack of appreciation between team members
People understand their contribution	People have little understanding of their role
Clear direction is found	Conflicting goals are found
Good communication exists	Mixed messages and little understanding
An even workload allowing for individual skills/abilities	Work is spread unevenly
Teams knows other team members skills/abilities	Little understanding exists on what makes the team tick
Work environment is conductive to good performance	Physical environment prevents good performance

The leaders and managers are, ultimately, the ones who can make the difference in how the culture "works". Total culture can provide the holistic perspective that can really transform and reshape organisations.

PART 4
SYSTEMS & PROBLEMS

"The same problems keep happening and no matter what we do, the system beats us."

The "system" referred to in this quotation is obviously a large and imposed system (whether organisational, or more broadly political, social, or economic). This type of system, with both structure and process, will be:

- Dynamic and non-linear with many interfaces
- Interlinked and interdependent with many dependencies
- Unpredictable and uncertain with consistent variability.

Compartmentalising all of the individual parts will not help, as putting things into boxes will most likely mean that we will lose the system's meaning. We must therefore see and think about:

- the whole of the structure and the processes
- the total organisational culture

- the purpose of the system (what it is supposed to do)
- the associated power and people aspects

15

PROBLEM-SOLVING

In a traditional problem-solving approach, we analyse by breaking down into parts and look at each part separately. This is essentially a reductionist approach and in the case of a complex system it may give sub-optimal solutions. For example, we may fix only one part but, we still have recurring problems and these may now have been made worse. In changing one part only, we now have the overall system working in a different way; all of the other ignored parts are now reacting differently with the one part we have changed.

With a systems problem-solving approach, we analyse by seeing the interactions in and between all of the parts. We take a more expansive holistic approach that involves us looking at complex problems with not too obvious solutions. We are aiming to use systems thinking to give us a total system solution.

16

SYSTEMS THINKING

"As a person thinks, then so they are"

"If you think you can or think you can't, you are right"

We do tend not to question our own thinking (or try consciously to change it). Once we have learnt something, then we will behave habitually. As we have explored more fully in The Learning Toolkit, to change behaviour we may have to look at the attitudes, thinking, values and beliefs that underpin the behaviour.

However, to see something happening, we have to know what to look for and this can be difficult with complex systems. Systems thinking will therefore help us to look into the complex dynamics that are created by people. Systems thinking will show "the big picture".

17

MENTAL MODELS

The real problem here, however, is that what often prevents us from seeing the big picture is that we are conditioned in our thinking. We have "mental models" as illustrated in the following diagram:

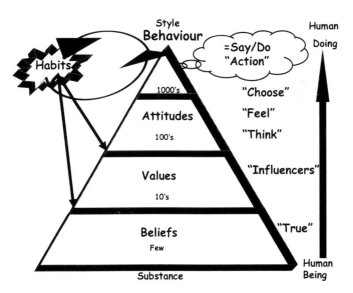

Our "reality" and perspectives come from our attitudes, values beliefs.

If different views are suggested or occur to us, then these views are either rejected or accepted; if they are accepted, then our mental models are changed.

Different perspectives can mean a widened mental model and our behaviour can then become habitual; we can now do things "without thinking" or "automatically". What we do or say is visible action that is underpinned by the more invisible attitudes, values and beliefs. Changing our attitudes, values and beliefs may, however, be difficult and uncomfortable, especially with deep-rooted habits.

We therefore have many shapers to our mental maps and our thinking. These include all of the following influences:

- Brain sides: Logical left and creative right
- Mind: Conscious and unconscious
- Memory: Short, working, and long-term
- Sight, sound and senses

Whilst these have all been covered more fully in The Learning Toolkit, it is worth noting here that the brain sides' styles of thinking and feeling are analogous to systems thinking.

The logical left brain is essentially convergent and reductionist "head" thinking that is ordered to think and analyse, then act and then feel. However, the creative right brain is more a divergent "heart" feeler/thinker that is ordered to first feel, then analyse, then act.

Logical left-brain people will therefore:

- Prefer written, mathematical, science-based approaches
- Favour objective, linear thinking, short-term views
- Break things down into parts
- Be analytical, step-by-step "head" thinkers
- Employ rational "facts"-based reasoning that converges
- In summary – analyse, act, then feel

Creative right-brain people will therefore:

- Prefer musical, art/visual approaches
- Favour subjective, wholes/parallel processing, longer-term views
- See the "big picture"
- Be creative, free flowing "heart" thinkers
- Use emotional "feelings" synthesis that diverges
- In summary – feel, analyse, then act

As it is people who operate companies, it is the leaders and managers who in turn will create what I have called, left or right brain companies:

Left-brain companies can be summarised as follows:

- Task-based, short-term
- Problems often reoccur as only the symptoms are treated ("band aid" solutions)
- Make profits by making/selling products or services
- Look "inside out"
- The way forward is with science/technology
- "The numbers speak for themselves"
- Incremental results/parts
- Functional silo structures, top down

Right-brain companies can be summarised as follows:

- People-based, long-term
- Problems are tackled by looking at the cause /thinking
- Make people first and before products-services
- Look "outside in"
- The way forward is by motivating/empowering people
- "It is how we connect together that is important"
- Holistic results/parts
- Cross functional and bottom up

Some of the consequences to these divisions are that financial decisions may be remote from the actual doing and are taken "for their own sake" ignoring the implications. There is no effective managing on the right side. There is no effective connection between the inputs, the process and the outputs.

This often results in short-term financial decisions that cause longer-term instabilities. Problems may be only picked up later, when the figures are available. There is no effective management as the root causes are being hidden and are not being acknowledged.

The right-brain company, however, takes time to set up. With its emphasis on feelings more than facts, then proof with objective figures is difficult and with no common financial language, explanations to others are not always going to be easy.

We are back again to the hard and soft values we explored earlier. Now this is not to say that each of these "ideal-typical" brain divisions is mutually exclusive; the reality is often a balance between the two – what Senge called "creative tension." In trying to find this right balance and blend of hard systems and objectivity with soft systems and subjectivity:

- Projects are assessed with cost/benefit analysis and measurement, but final decisions may be taken using gut feelings and intuition – a combination of the "head" with the "heart"
- Demand forecasting is statistically based, but

also employs sales force market intuition and "gut feel"

The conceptual framework of systems thinking does allow for both objective facts and subjective feelings. It does this by concentrating on the inter-relationships that drive the systems behaviour. It recognises that it is people who can leverage and influence the relationships and therefore the system – such leverage often actually coming from changing the mental models which are supporting the system structure.

In mental models, "perception is reality" – and what we see and think about determines what we do. To change these mental models, we must commit to changing ourselves. More simply, "if it is to be, then it's down to me."

PART 5
SYSTEMS THINKING AND ORGANISATIONAL IMPROVEMENTS

This section of the book is to be read with a health and thinking warning. Think carefully which aspects might apply to your own organisation, and how.

By now, you will hopefully have seen that systems thinking is not a rigid set of "doing-it-this-one-way" thinking and is more about "mixing-the-doing-and-being" thinking. It is not about blindly applying tools but is all about changing our thinking.

So with this in mind, let us now consider some important aspects of systems thinking which will influence how effectively the organisation can operate.

18

POSITIVE AND NEGATIVE FEEDBACK

Effective systems thinking views the causes of behaviour as coming from circular positive and negative feedback or influences. (It should be noted that the words positive and negative do not mean good or bad.) These are:

- Positive and reinforcing feedback. This is where one thing reinforces another thing. Changes to a system come back and amplify and force a change. This change is growth, or collapse/decay, in both cases moving the system away from its initial starting point.
  - Negative and balancing feedback is where one thing varies another thing, in the opposite direction. Changes feed back to oppose the original change; they dampen the effect and give less of the original action. Negative

feedback balances and gives stability as it resists attempts to change it.

Importantly, the feedback may be time-lagged and delayed. We can also have variability meaning unpredictability. As an example, enter here complexity theory with its well-known illustration of a butterfly flapping its wings in the Amazon Basin, causing a hurricane three days later in Hong Kong.

In dependent and variable processes and systems, what happens here may affect what happens there. Unfortunately the here and there may not be seen as being connected, or both part of "our" system. We may not have knowledge of the dependencies, or we may just not have the visibility of the process.

19

WHOLES AND NOT JUST THE PARTS

Systems thinking sees wholes and not just the parts. It sees the relationships and connections alluded to above, where small changes in one part of a system area may cause big changes elsewhere. This can mean that when we look wider, greater possibilities are found.

An example might be making an overall reduction in costs, while the service levels *increase*. The following is an example of exactly this type of change which I have witnessed. As a result of changes implemented in this company's supply chain:

- Raw materials costs fell to 71.5% of their previous level
- Production costs increased to 115.6%
- Finished goods stock costs reduced to 66.4%
- Transport costs increased to 102.8%
- Total costs were reduced to 97.3%
- Service levels increased from 90 to 98%

Thus, while some individual costs increased, the overall costs decreased. Meanwhile the service was improved. We cannot imagine that the people in charge of Production and Transport would have sponsored such a change on their own. Unless a total more holistic supply chain view was taken, then such double wins on cost and service improvements may not have been found.

20

LEVELS AND RATES

The Dynamics of Systems thinking are levels and rates.

Levels in systems thinking are levels of resources. Examples of resources that are used as inputs into processes are the **7 Ms**:

- Manpower or people
- Motivation levels
- Materials and consumables (for example, energy, water, electric)
- Machinery, plant and equipment
- Money and cash
- Methods of working
- Minutes (time – that most precious infinite resource that once used, has gone, never to return)

These resources may be:

- plentiful or rare

- physical or abstract
- renewable (like profit) or non-renewable (like oil)
- accumulated – for example, a financial balance sheet that shows the money in the organisation, the raw material stocks held to enable production, or the finished goods stocks to facilitate availability to customers

Rates are the flow of resources that cause action. However, we need a decision to cause the action and, in turn, we first need information to make the decision.

21

STRUCTURE DRIVES BEHAVIOUR

Systems thinking identifies repeatable patterns in a process, and recognises the way that structure drives behaviour. The behaviour outputs may be

- growth or decay
- goal-seeking
- variability/oscillations
- linked positive and negative feedback which will respond to each other and limit growth

We will look briefly below at ways that structure drives behaviour, in the context of organisational structure.

Organisations and structure and behaviour

An organisation is a human activity system of which the structure is just one part. A consultant's overview of an organisation is provided by the McKinsey's 7S Model that shows the following are involved:

- **S**trategy: the vision and plan
- **S**ystems: the ways of doing things
- **S**taff: the people
- **S**kills: the know-how and intellectual property
- **S**tyle: the management styles and communication
- **S**hared Values: the culture and ethos
- **S**tructure: the relationships and functions

All of these have already been discussed, apart from structure.

Organisation structure

A definition of organisation structure is as follows:

"The planned design of company structure which shows the relationships and functions to be performed by each individual, so that the company works effectively towards known objectives."

The organisation structure therefore has a major influence on the running of the organisation and the people within it. For example, it is said:

"The structure holds up and supports everything we do."

In this latter sense, the structure provides stability with fixed and known rules and procedures. Within the structural framework, the operational processes of the organisation take place and here we will find variability, dependency and interfaces. These may be found within all of the following:

- Purpose or strategy – the structure is designed to achieve this purpose
- Methods and technology used
- Information and decision-making process
- Supplier and customer separation
- Scale and range of activities and resources
- People's knowledge and skills, including their management "style" – for example, commanding and controlling or coaching and empowering
- Legal status, accountability and sources of finance

People operate dynamically and contractually in the structure. Most of these contracts are not hard value based or legal ones, but are informal psychological contracts with soft values that are not written down; they are frequently changed and are determined by a mix of logic and emotions.

Any structural changes made will impact on the informal contracts as well as the formal ones. The chosen structure should be one that promotes the peak performance of the people, processes and products or services being delivered to customers.

It should ensure the opposite of the following identified common **weaknesses** in structures:

- Too many levels of authority, leading to slow communication and decision-making
- Too many people to manage, leading to poor communication, ignored improvements, feelings of isolation
- One department view rules – for example, a belief that says the Finance department are the "kings" – whereas a systems view of an organisation will see that it is the key cross-functional processes that are the most important
- Top-down view – for example, there may be a belief that the published organisational chart reflects the *only* (or *best*) way to work

PART 6
IMPROVEMENT METHODS

22

SYSTEMS THINKING AND IMPROVEMENTS

As we have seen in the previous sections of this book, in order to really change performance it is necessary to apply the principles of systems thinking, and change the system or structure which underpins the relevant actions. Indeed, the changes to the structure can be quite small and may still lead to significant improvements. Large-scale efforts may not be needed.

Indeed, Peter Senge has observed that problems are nearly always caused by the way we do things and that one small policy change may solve many problems easily.

However, the action which needs to be changed is often far away in time and place from where the problem appears and without the benefit of effective systems thinking the connection between the problem and the action may never be identified. Even if it is identified, without the right approach the action may be pushed in wrong direction, thereby intensifying the problem.

Systems thinking is fundamental to change, and is itself subject to continuing change and re-evaluation. No improvement strategy will ever remain the same for the long run due to the ever-changing dynamic market and external demands. The following diagram illustrates the iterative nature, of performance improvement.

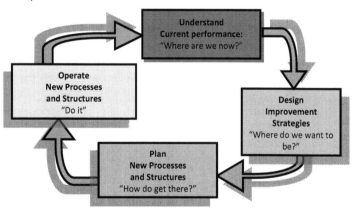

It is essential to appreciate that making changes will mean changing both the system and the thinking. Systems thinking is about applying principles, not tools; feedback, wholes, variabilities, structures and dynamics must be considered.

An excessive reliance on methods and tools can

be dangerous. For example, many organisations have been unsuccessful in introducing the acclaimed Toyota Production System, purely because they concentrate on the explicit tools and not on the implicit principles. They want the easy tools but not the thinking behind them.

We are back to the earlier section on Mental Models where "perception is reality" and what we see and think about determines what we do.

To make continuous improvements, systems principles need applying correctly in a continuous series of controlled experiments that is also a continual cycle of learning and changing.

23

SYSTEMS ANALYSIS

This is a questioning approach adapted from Balle. It may need several iterations, with each iteration revealing deeper detail. This is the sequence:

1) What is the system?

- Can we map the structures and dynamics?
- Are the feedback loops, dependencies, variabilities and interfaces understood?
- How does the system look, feel, sound?
- What is its history?

2) Who are the players?

- Who is involved?
- Who will be affected by this?
- What is their logic?
- What are their motivation/interests?
- What action do they take?

3) What is the growth engine?

- What positive loop reinforces/drives the system?
- What is in people's minds?
- Where are we now?
- Where do we want to be?
- How are we going to get there?

4) What are the main limiting factors?

- What are the main balancing negative loops?
- Is there some rare resource we are ignoring?

5) Expand the frame

- What is the next link?
- What is the previous one?
- Is there a loop we are not seeing?

6) Operational action points

- Where can we find the leverage?
- Has it been shown by exposing the limiting factors?
- What practical action can we take?

7) Communicate

- Get buy-in

24

CHECKLAND AND SOFT SYSTEMS

This is a qualitative approach to deal with problem situations in socio-political-human activity systems (aka soft systems). It gives a structure and specific techniques to look at complex situations and will force a non-technical solution. It uses the six steps set out below – again, this process may need several iterations.

1) Unstructured review of the problem system

This might be achieved by use of rich pictures, these being visual representations and can take many forms like mind-maps combined with flowcharts and process charts, etc. These show the boundaries, structures, information flows, etc., with the human activities.

2) Basic/root definition using CATWOE descriptors

The idea here is to come up with a definition of the system. The following descriptors provide a checklist to make sure that everything is covered:

- **C**ustomers – everyone who may gain benefits from the system

- **A**ctors – those who transform inputs into outputs and those who perform the defined activities of the system

- **T**ransformation process – the process used to converts inputs to outputs

- **W**eltanschauung (German word for world view) – makes the transformation "meaningful" for someone

- **O**wner – those that have power start, close or veto the system

- **E**nvironmental constraints – external elements to be considered such as policies, legal constraints, ethics, etc.

3) Conceptual models

Conceptual models are your representation, following from (2) above, of how the system behaves, and should structure the interrelationships that are driving the system's behaviour. Often a detailed visual representation is sufficient.

4) Compare (3) with (2)

5) Examine feasible, desirable changes

6) Take action to improve (1)

25

LEAN SYSTEMS

Much has been written about the advantages of lean thinking, and lean systems, which encourage the total elimination of waste in all aspects of business management, and the development of responsive just-in-time business systems.

Author and business consultant John Seddon has written about the application of these principles to systems thinking. In his own words, "When systems thinking is applied to the design and management of work, it is both interesting and profitable."

The following extract from an online article by John Seddon contains many important messages on making improvements and stresses the importance of using systems thinking to do this.

Change means changing the system

Change for improved performance means changing the system. When features of a traditional management system are left in place, they undermine (or, minimally, compete with) quality principles and practices. If change doesn't change the system, the system doesn't change.

Any intervention in a system which does not change the thinking will produce no change. This is why training in quality techniques fails to improve performance over the medium term (and sometimes even in the short term). The principles and practices of traditional, hierarchical, functional management, which today constitute the accepted norm, are antithetical to quality principles and practices. This is not just a matter of attitude and belief. The everyday practical matters which managers work with are different in a quality organisation in very real ways. A systems view of the organisation leads to different measures used in a different way. It means designing work according to different principles.

A systems view of an organisation starts from the outside-in. How does this organisation look to its customers? How easy are we to do business with? (One company used this as its slogan but was very difficult to do business with. It was the customers who had to manage them to get anything done). The starting place for understanding the organisation as a system is to be able to predict what will happen next week if nothing changes.

Implications for management

It is only when people's view of how to do work changes that their behaviour changes. Changing the system means taking out things which have been limiting or damaging current performance. For example, removing activity measures, arbitrary targets and ceasing to manage performance through budgets; changing structure and processes to enable them to better achieve their purpose. Managers will only take such radical action if and when they appreciate that their traditional means of control in fact give them less control: managing costs cause's costs.

> When the organisation is understood as a system, the inappropriateness of such practices becomes stark. It is a major source of motivation for action. Action means "doing the right thing"; putting in place the right "system conditions" to ensure that performance is managed from a strong base of understanding. Deming taught the Japanese to manage their organisations as systems. In four years they out-achieved his expectations. When people work from theory they learn. What Deming gave them was a theory of management which started from the premise that the organisation is a system. Organisations of the future will be learning because their people, the people who do the work, will be learning. But that will only happen as fast as we change the way we run organisations. Without doubt it is the right thing to do.
>
> Source: John Seddon, "Systems thinking - management by doing the right thing", www.lean-service.com

Perhaps one day all organisations will be continually improving and be continually learning. This is the promise of systems thinking which is all about applying principles and not tools, and which (as we have seen) considers feedback, wholes, variabilities, structures and dynamics.

To repeat a point made earlier – in order to make continuous improvements, systems principles need to be applied in a continuous series of controlled experiments, which is also itself a continual cycle of learning and changing. This must be the ultimate objective of the systems thinker.

CONCLUSION

In the introduction we highlighted several areas that managers can work on to improve productivity. These are shown again below with a link, (in brackets), to the appropriate Business Toolkit.

- Insufficient planning and control (dealt with in this Systems Toolkit)
- Inadequate supervision (see the Team Management Toolkit)
- Poor morale (see the Motivation Toolkit)
- Inappropriate people development (see the Developing People toolkit)
- IT related problems (included in this Systems Toolkit)
- Ineffective communication (see the Communication Toolkit)
- Poor Human Resources Management procedures (see the Human Resources Toolkit)
- Poor customer service (see the Customer Service Toolkit)
- Poor training/learning for specific skills and procedures (see the Learning Toolkit)

Readers are encouraged to take advantage of the complete list of toolkits, which complement each other to provide a comprehensive portfolio of concise pocket guides to improved personal and business performance.

REFERENCES

Balle, Michael, 1994: "Managing with Systems Thinking", McGraw Hill

Checkland, Peter, 1981: "Systems Thinking, Systems Practice", Wiley

Drucker, Peter, 2004: "The Daily Drucker", Harper Business

Harvey Jones, John, 1995: "All Together Now", William Heinemann

Senge, Peter, 1990: "The Fifth Discipline", Century

Seddon, John: "Systems thinking - management by doing the right thing", www.lean-service.com

Seddon John, 2003: "Freedom from Command & Control", Vanguard Education Limited

Welch, Jack, with John Byrne, 2001 and 2003: "Jack, straight from the gut", Headline Book Publishing

Nick Read, CEO Vodaphone UK in "The Sunday Times" 1 April 2007

ABOUT THE AUTHOR

My own journey to "today", whilst an individual one, did not happen, thankfully, without other people's involvement. I smile when I remember so many helpful people. So to anyone who has ever had contact with me, then please be assured you will have contributed to my own learning, growing and developing.

After spending over 30 years in commercial private sector service industries, I entered the logistics and supply chain people development business. After nine years as a Director of Training, I then choose to become a freelance independent mentor/coach, trainer and consultant. This built on my past operational and strategic experience - gained in the UK and Nigeria - and my particular interest in the "people issues" of management processes.

Trading under the name of Learn and Change Limited, I currently enjoy working all over the UK and also on four other continents, principally in Africa and the Middle East, but also in the Far East and South America. In addition to my training activities, I am also involved in one-to-one coaching/mentoring, consulting, writing, assessing and examining for professional institutes' and university qualifications.

I can be contacted at stuart@learnandchange.com or by visiting www.learnandchange.com. I welcome any comments.

Other books in the series

THE BUSINESS STRATEGY TOOLKIT
by David Cotton

Many senior managers and company leaders are blissfully ignorant of what strategy really is. They use the word "strategy" constantly without ever clearly defining their own. They berate their staff for being task focused and working in silos, but are unable to articulate a strategy sufficiently clearly to change this.

The Business Strategy Toolkit is a concise and highly practical guide designed to give managers the tools to elicit their own strategy, to communicate it in the most appropriate ways to their staff, and to look at practical ways to implement that strategy.

Paperback • 160pp • £5.99

THE COMMUNICATION TOOLKIT
by Stuart Emmett

Communication is perhaps the most important management skill – and often the most overlooked. Poor communication can create a major barrier to improving performance. Good communication creates immediate benefits both in terms of personal achievement and in terms of team performance as a whole.

This practical manual provides essential advice and techniques for anyone wanting to brush up their communication skills. It will provide inspiration, insight, and above all methodology for improved communication in business.

Paperback • 104pp • £5.99

THE CUSTOMER SERVICE TOOLKIT
by Stuart Emmett

Customers are what really drive an organisation; lose your customers and you lose your business. Good customer service is therefore essential to the survival of any business, and yet many companies provide little or no training in this essential discipline – often with disastrous results.

This practical manual provides essential advice and techniques for anyone wanting to brush up their customer service skills. It will provide inspiration, insight, and above all methodology for improved customer service.

Paperback • 118pp • £5.99

THE HUMAN RESOURCES TOOLKIT
by Richard McNamara

Human resources management is at the heart of every successful business. It deals with all aspects of staff recruitment, development and welfare, as well as the thornier aspects of disciplinary procedure. Yet the HR function is often not fully appreciated or understood by line managers.

This practical manual explains the HR function and shows line managers and others how they can get the most out of their relationship with their HR departments. It will provide inspiration, insight and above all methodology for improved HR.

Paperback • 106pp • £5.99

THE LEARNING TOOLKIT
by Stuart Emmett

Just about everything we ever do must be learnt. However, learning is not an automatic process; it is a skill – and one which many of us lose as we grow older. In a business context, the ability to learn new techniques, absorb new knowledge, or come to grips with new aspects of a changing job, is absolutely vital to our performance. Yet surprisingly few people stop to think "How can I learn better?"

This practical manual provides essential advice and techniques for anyone wanting to improve their learning skills. It will provide inspiration, insight, and above all methodology for improved learning.

Paperback • 108pp • £5.99

THE MOTIVATION TOOLKIT
by Stuart Emmett

Motivation is absolutely key to performance. In this respect, the ability to motivate staff is an essential management skill. Yet this is an area of management often overlooked in basic management training. The nature of motivation is complex and must be learned – as must the techniques and processes for achieving it.

This practical manual provides essential advice and techniques for anyone wanting to improve the motivation of their staff. It will provide inspiration, insight, and above all methodology for motivation.

Paperback • 108pp • £5.99

THE PEOPLE DEVELOPMENT TOOLKIT
by Stuart Emmett

People are the single most important asset of an organisation. To make sure you keep your best employees, and maximise their contribution to the business, it is essential to help them to develop to the best of their ability. This requires a comprehensive programme of employee development including systematic and continuous training, personal mentoring, and much more besides.

This practical manual provides essential advice and techniques for anyone wanting to implement a continuous professional development (CPD) programme, or to improve their people development procedures. It will provide inspiration, insight, and above all methodology for effective people development.

Paperback • 104pp • £5.99

THE TEAM MANAGEMENT TOOLKIT
by Stuart Emmett

Good team management can make the difference between success and failure in the achievement of a given task. Yet few managers are trained in this essential skill. How do teams function, and how can they be managed to optimise both individual and team performance?

This practical manual provides essential advice and techniques for anyone wanting to brush up on their team management skills. It will provide inspiration, insight, and above all methodology for improved team management.

Paperback • 110pp • £5.99